CONTAINERS BEYOND THE HYPE

CONTAINERS BEYOND THE HYPE

First print edition, December 2015

ISBN: 978-0-9970236-1-9

Cover design, layout and illustrations: Anna Chakravorty and Suchakra Sharma

Acknowledgements

The history of Linux containers is a long and circuitous one, as is my association with the underlying technology. In its course, it introduced me to a number of outstanding individuals from Columbia University, Hewlett Packard Labs, Meiosys, IBM Research, Altiscale, and most recently AppOrbit. These people have contributed immensely to my learning. Much of what I wrote in this book are insights and experiences I gathered while working with them.

First and foremost, I want to thank Jason Nieh, my Ph.D. advisor at Columbia University, for guiding me through the conception and initial implementation stages of container and checkpoint/restore technologies. There are several others I wish to thank. John Janakiraman, Yoshio Turner, and Renato Santos worked with me at HP Labs on extending containers to support distributed checkpointing. Jason Donahue exposed me to the fascinating process of transforming a sophisticated technology like container live-migration into a product and a business at Meiosys. Mark Dean inspired me to continue my work on record/replay of containers and to resume my Ph.D. work after the acquisition of Meiosys by IBM. Raymie Stata presented me with the opportunity to apply containers to a complex real-world application ecosystem. Finally, I want to thank my cofounders at AppOrbit for the opportunity to give business expression to some of these learnings.

Over the years, containers as a technology has branched into different forms across various platforms. The experience I share in this book is presented from the specific vantage point of the roles I served during the evolution of this technology. Countless engineers from many companies have brought containers to its current breadth and level of adoption. If not for their tremendous work, containers would have remained a prototype. This book is dedicated to their effort.

Contents

A Brief History of Containers: From Reality to Hype 10

Organization of the Book 15

Software Is From Heaven, Applications are from Dependency Hell 16

What exactly is an application? 19

Interfaces versus Intrafaces 20

Containers 22

The Art of Virtualization and the Science of Containerization 24

Resource Anomalies 27

Application State 28

Namespaces 31

Application State Machine 34

The Containerization Continuum 38

Chroot, Jails, and the CLONE_NEWNS Artifact 42

Unikernels 42

Virtual Machines 43

Virtual Machines and Their Unwelcome Guests 44

VMs: Wrong Abstraction for Applications 51

Containers: Scaled-in Virtualization for Scale-out Applications 55

Future of Containers: From Hype Back to Reality 56

Microservices: Containers All the Way Down 60

Role of Containers in Data Center Operating Systems 61

Container Runtimes 64

Looking Ahead 67

I

A Brief History of Containers: From Reality to Hype

\\. It was a chilly winter morning 10 years ago in Somers, New York. The small upstate town is dominated by the sprawling buildings of IBM corporate headquarters. For a few of us, the hard work of the past several years was going to come to a head as we walked into the campus' main building with a couple of bulky servers. They had a self contained setup of the system that we were going to demo to IBM's senior executive team. Ironically, the technology in those boxes could remove the need to carry preconfigured physical hardware by making them readily available on-demand. That was also precisely the reason for IBM's interest in our small upstart, Meiosys. IBM was rapidly executing on its on-demand strategy. HP called it *utility computing* and Sun Microsystems called it *N1* but they were all precursors to what we call cloud today.

The demo entailed repeated live migration of a containerized three-tier application back and forth between two servers while it was under load from the TPC-C benchmark.The technology was advanced.It not only virtualized the application using a fundamentally efficient abstraction but also supported sophisticated features such as live-migration and coordinated checkpoint-restore of distributed applications. The application, including all its state was wrapped in a thin layer of virtualization that we called the *container*.

"The technology was advanced. It not only virtualized the application using a fundamentally efficient abstraction but also supported sophisticated features such as live-migration and coordinated checkpoint-restore of distributed applications."

Based on principles and techniques that originated at Columbia University and Hewlett Packard Labs in early 2000s, the container abstraction decoupled the application from the underlying system by encapsulating its state into a self-contained unit. The state of each application resource, including the state of its runtime memory and the state of its open socket connections, was captured and live-migrated to the target machine. Not one dropped connection! It was an awesome feat of research and engineering. Following its acquisition by IBM in 2005, Meiosys' technology became the basis for containers on Linux and IBM AIX operating systems.

The technology was sophisticated and robust but it required custom changes to the kernel that spanned almost every subsystem. Implementing the changes in AIX was relatively fast. However, getting the changes merged into mainstream Linux kernel was a rather long and deliberate process. Even though a fully functioning patch was available, it was too big. It had to be washed, dried and chopped into bite size pieces for community consumption. After over a decade of community effort, most changes made their way into the kernel. However, the changes were now implemented as independent features in various kernel subsystems. The freshly minted features were not easy to configure and use them together. Although many companies began experimenting internally and embedding them into their products, out-of-the-box user space support to tie them all into easily deployable containers was inadequate.

This was a clear opportunity for DotCloud, one of the early users of containers that keenly understood the value of the technology. With the center of gravity of virtual machine vendors shifting away from core virtualization to storage and higher layers of the management stack, the conditions were ripe for containers. DotCloud created the Docker open source project with the explicit charter to hide the complexity of the kernel features through a simple user interface combined with a repository of container images that can be readily deployed. To the developers used to virtual machine based packaging, it was like magic to see dispensable OS environments come up and go instantly. Docker was an immediate success.

Much has been written about Docker containers since. Docker's model quickly became popular. What has been a simmering activity in niche kernel circles for over a decade has quite suddenly become the active focus of companies like Google, HP, IBM and Microsoft. Some are touting containers as the "next generation of virtualization" and "technology of the decade." Containers are almost becoming synonymous to Docker. Few technologies have seen this kind of adoption rate.

Technologies rarely move so quickly from conception to viral adoption. While Docker and its usage model has been the first highly visible introduction of containers to the industry, the underlying technology itself is deep and broad. Containers are just beginning to transition out of their long incubation and they are still in an early stage of adoption. Many new interesting usage models and capabilities are still to emerge.

What took so long?

One reason for the long gestation period is virtual machines. Early on, virtual machines, particularly VMware, met the requirement to consolidate Windows workloads onto fewer, more beefy SMP Intel servers. By the time containers were introduced as a product, virtual machines had grown beyond the initial consolidation usecase to a general application management layer. Many usage models where containers would have been a much better fit were being served with virtual machines. Interestingly, that gave containers time to build up an extensive capability set, all to be eventually released with a big splash.

Organization of the Book

This book captures a balanced view of containers, that goes beyond the current hype. Beginning with a discussion of the fundamental and long-standing problems that containers were designed to address, the book provides a conceptual framework that describes containers as a technology. Rather than prescriptive models, it presents the grass-root use cases that are emerging. Finally, it describes the interesting ways in which containers are intersecting with key trends, hinting at the technology gaps and the advanced capabilities that could evolve in the future.

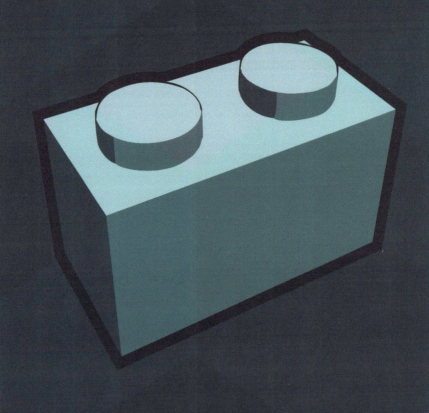

II

Software
Is From Heaven,
Applications are From
Dependency Hell

\\. Software and applications may appear to be synonymous terms, but they are quite different concepts. Alan Turing defined software elegantly with his eponymous machine that rigorously describes computer logic. Any individual program can be precisely modeled as a Turing machine. Applications, however, are a higher level fabrication consisting of numerous interdependent layers of logic spanning from application code to external libraries, operating system code, and processor-level stored procedures. Although we have been talking about applications for many years, what we refer to as an application doesn't really have a formal definition.

"Although we have been talking about applications for many years, what we refer to as an application doesn't really have a formal definition."

What exactly is an application?

- Is it the executable? But it may require external libraries to function.
- Is it the binary together with the libraries? But it could have associated configuration, system libraries and external state which is implicitly a part of the application.
- Is it the installation package like an RPM? But the installation package is not really runnable as an application until installed. Once a package is installed however, the application becomes an inseparable part of the platform substrate without a well defined boundary.
- Is it the operating system processes that represent the application? But there could be other required code and shared state that is external to those processes.

While Turing's model describes software, it is not quite appropriate to define modern applications. It models software in general but it doesn't really apply to today's environments consisting of myriads of software components interconnected in complex configurations. At some point along the way from the original Turing machine model to today's world of complex software, applications have evolved as independent entities but have escaped definition.

INTERFACES VERSUS *INTRAFACES*

With growing popularity of web service models over the last several years, we have been obsessed with interfaces as an industry. Applications expose services through their external interfaces. The expected external view of an application in terms of its interface contracts is typically well-defined. However, the application's internal structure as an entity of the operating system and the interface between the application and the underlying system are not well defined. There is no boundary around what state constitutes an application. Without such a boundary, designing and maintaining consistent interfaces across environments is impossible.

It's About Broken Intrafaces

Lack of proper definition around an application has caused many problems over the years in the form of broken interfaces. It has been particularly difficult to ensure that applications can run correctly across different environments. Applications are typically designed to anticipate and accept the behavior of their environment. However they often encounter unexpected landscapes and mysteriously break.

An unexpected state of file system artifacts is one of the most common sources of broken application interfaces. Here are some examples: One application destructively upgrades a base package on the file system, overwriting files required by another application. A required application component is missing altogether. A stale version of a system library is running on a backward-incompatible kernel interface. A configuration file is incorrectly modified or accidentally deleted during maintenance.

Some unexpected dependencies could cause failures at runtime. The IP address of the host may have changed because the DHCP lease could not be renewed, rendering the service unreachable. Or there could be a discrepancy in the response from a co-deployed service.

These problems have been so prevalent and persistent that they are referred to as *dependency hell*. Operations teams go to great lengths to avoid unforeseen application dependencies. Sometimes several staging instances of a production environment are dedicated to testing. Configuration management has arisen as a separate practice in response to the problem. While configuration management tools and practices may be OK for general hygiene, they are often inadequate, error prone, and impose high operation burden.

"Containers offer an elegant abstraction to achieve what otherwise requires strict austerity and operational discipline to maintain the sterility of application environments with fragile dependencies."

Containers offer an elegant abstraction to achieve what otherwise requires strict austerity and operational discipline to maintain the sterility of application environments with fragile dependencies. In contrast to complex and implicit interdependencies among applications, system libraries, and the OS in a traditional application environment, a container defines an application as a decoupled entity and transforms it into a composable block. (See Figure 1.) Through a thin layer of software at the boundary of the application and the operating system, a container creates a virtual environment that decouples the application and systematically eliminates its dependencies on the underlying system. To an application running within a container, the environment is indistinguishable from an independent and private operating system instance.

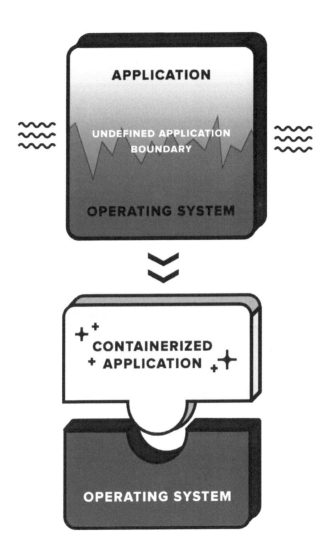

Figure 1. A container defines an application as a decoupled entity and transforms it into a composable block

III

The Art of
Virtualization and
The Science of
Containerization

\\. Containers are backed by a sound conceptual structure that is based on a study of applications, their internal relationships with underlying environment, the nature of problems that arise due to a poorly defined application boundary, and the requirements that must be met in order to define applications as individual entities decoupled from underlying systems. Containers lend definition to the otherwise abstract notion of an application. This chapter explores the science behind how containers define and decouple applications.

"Containers lend definition to the otherwise abstract notion of an application."

RESOURCE ANOMILIES

Decoupling applications from the platform requires addressing three types of anomalies with respect to their resources:

- **Resource consistency.** Applications expect that the names of resources they need remain consistent. For example, an application would fail if the network interface used by the application acquires a new IP address or if the location of a required configuration file changes.

- **Resource conflicts.** Applications expect that they have private access to the resources they need. For example, an application would fail if the required network port is already in use or if another application overwrites a shared library it needs.

- **Resource dependencies.** Applications expect that the resources they need are accessible to them. For example, an application would fail if a network service it needs is unreachable or if its data is not available to it.

These anomalies are defined conservatively. Some applications may continue to run even with inconsistent references, conflicts or dependencies, but in general, these issues must be reconciled to decouple the application from its platform.

APPLICATION STATE

To understand how containers address these anomalies, it's necessary to consider the variety of states that comprise an application. These range from the simple runtime state of the CPU registers to the application data residing on the backend storage systems. Some states are necessarily private. For example, the state of the CPU registers of an application thread is private to the application by virtue of the operating system kernel mechanism that arbitrates access to it. Even though the physical CPU registers are shared by the applications and the kernel, the scheduler maintains a private copy of each application's state and virtualizes access to it. An application doesn't fail because of missing register contents or contents that have been unexpectedly changed under the covers. Only the owning thread can modify this state. In effect, the application runs within a private namespace of CPU registers offered by the operating system's thread abstraction.

Similarly, the memory state of an application process is private. Even though applications may share the same physical memory on a machine, the virtual memory subsystem of the kernel virtualizes access to it through hardware support in the form of page tables. In effect, the application runs within a private namespace of memory provided by the process abstraction through its virtual memory address space.

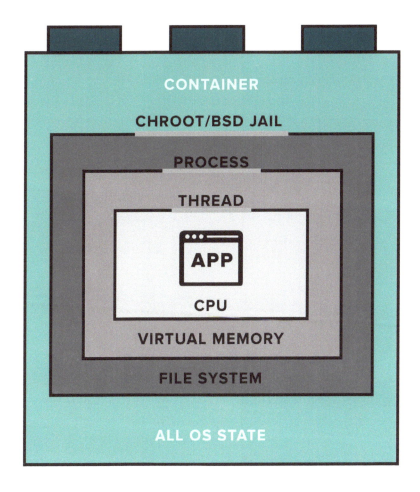

Figure 2. Layers of application state and their progressively inclusive encapsulations provide progressively higher levels of decoupling from the platform

The scope of the encapsulation can be extended further as shown in Figure 2. In fact, tools such as `chroot` fit the same model as well. *Chroot* and *BSD Jails* encapsulate the state of the file system in addition to other lower-level state. Some may liken containers to `chroot`. But it is inaccurate and misleading. Containers are no more like `chroot` than virtual machines are like logical volumes. Logical volumes may virtualize storage but it is the comprehensive treatment of every machine resource that makes virtual machines what they are.

"Containers are no more like `chroot` than virtual machines are like logical volumes."

In contrast to earlier tools and abstractions that focus on specific pieces of application state, the container model takes a holistic approach to systematically address the entire state of the application. It decouples an application from the underlying operating system by extending encapsulation to all resources of the application. It is this principled approach to identifying and decoupling application state around the stable operating system interface that makes containers the ideal abstraction for application virtualization. Containerization not only guarantees that the application can be consistently deployed and run on a variety of platforms but also provides sufficient decoupling to migrate a live application.

NAMESPACES

The container abstraction is based on a set of namespaces. A namespace is simply a collection of named objects. Each namespace represents a particular resource. (See Figure 3.) A resource namespace reconciles application's relationships with its environment with respect to that resource. It has the following three properties.

- It is self-contained. It represents a closure of the state of the respective resource required by the application to run correctly. That is, it aggregates all related pieces of the resource state into a self-contained unit such that external conflicts and dependencies are removed. For example, if a process within a process namespace forks a child process, the child process is also included within that namespace. When the parent process later queries the exit status of the child process, it would be readily available.

- It provides virtual names to the resources within the namespace, decoupled from their external identities to remove inconsistent references to those resources and conflicts in their names.

- It is immutable except through the execution of the application. The internal state of a namespace cannot be directly modified from outside. Immutability of a namespace is key to guaranteeing repeatability of application execution across environments.

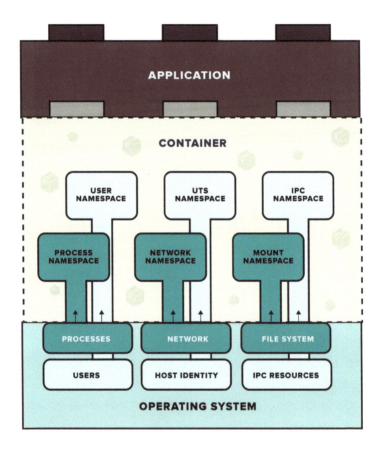

Figure 3. Containers project a subset of host resources to the application through a set of namespaces.

Even though the conceptual model of namespaces defines these properties, specific implementations may allow more relaxed primitives. Particularly, current Linux implementation allows directly modifying the state of the namespaces. For example, a user on the host, who is a part of the global namespace, would have access to the resources of all namespaces of the system. The user could directly modify application configuration files or other data within the file system namespace of a container, potentially causing undesirable interference and breaking the application. Even external processes along with any external dependencies they may have acquired during their external tenure are allowed to become part of a process namespace. The kernel itself doesn't forbid such incursions. Instead it is left to user space tools to enforce them.

Namespaces address unresolved interferences with external environment but they are not independent themselves. They depend on the operating system kernel interface. However, the dependency is now made clear and explicit. As long as the kernel interface is available, the container would run as expected. The linux implementation currently supports six namespaces, namely *PID* for process identifiers, *IPC* for resources related to interprocess communication, *UTS* for a private per-container host identity, *MNT* for a private file system view, NET for a private set of network resources and *USR* for user identifiers.

Resource Isolation and Cgroups

Resource namespaces naturally give rise to resource isolation and resource limits. Because namespaces form a boundary around the resources used by a containerized application, they provide a natural scope for the isolation of their resources and for enforcing limits on their usage. The *Cgroup* subsystem in Linux implements resource limits for namespaces and currently supports several resources including CPU, physical memory, and I/O bandwidth.

APPLICATION STATE MACHINE

Namespaces are static abstractions but the container itself is dynamic. It can be loosely modeled as a deterministic state machine that represents the application, with its internal state reflected by the state of the container's namespaces.

Repeatability

One of the key properties of a deterministic state machine is that it takes the same path each time, as long as it starts from the same initial state and the same inputs are presented. (See Figure 4.) In other words, the same version of an application will follow the same path each time it runs in an identical context consisting of the same versions of libraries and external state. In the case of containers, since namespaces are self-contained, all inputs to the application come from within the namespace and are guaranteed to be the same across environments because the required state is included with the container. Immutability and virtual names of namespaces ensure that no unexpected changes or references to the external environment are introduced.

An application's execution may take different paths due to intrinsic nondeterminism induced by system calls such as `gettimeofday()`. That application can still be considered deterministic at a coarser level because all those paths are valid. It is the unexpected changes to the state of container that need to be resolved. It is for that same reason that directly logging into a container is disallowed as a best practice.

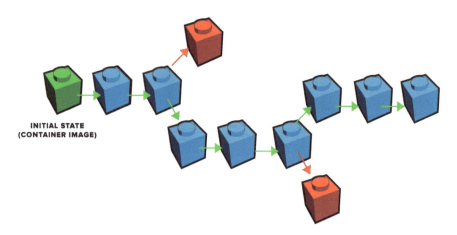

INITIAL STATE
(CONTAINER IMAGE)

Figure 4. Deterministic state machine model of a container showing the evolution of the container state as it executes.

Failures

Even though the state of namespaces is immutable, it may be modified in unexpected ways due to application bugs or failures. There are sophisticated checkpointing and logging techniques that can recover an application to a consistent state. A simpler approach to repeatable execution is to restart the state machine from its known initial state. The key here is to ensure that the container state machine is presented with the same initial state.

Container Image

The initial state of the container state machine is defined by the container image and consists of the initial state used to instantiate the container namespaces. In particular, the initial state specifies the file system hierarchy used to initialize the mount namespace of the container. It includes all binaries, configuration files needed by the application, and any user-specified data in the form of volumes. The initial state of the process namespace is specified as the executable from which the first process in the namespace is created. Some namespaces, such as the IPC namespace, are left blank. Others, such as the user namespace, are initialized with reasonable defaults.

The container is started by initializing the namespaces with the seed state specified by the container's image. The first process of the container is created from the application executable and added to the container's process namespace, jumpstarting the state machine.

The first process within the container can be any application binary in the container file system. It can even be the standard *init* system that brings up system services during operating system startup (**/sbin/init**). In this case, the container simply behaves like a machine. Containers running the entire *init* system are sometimes called system containers.

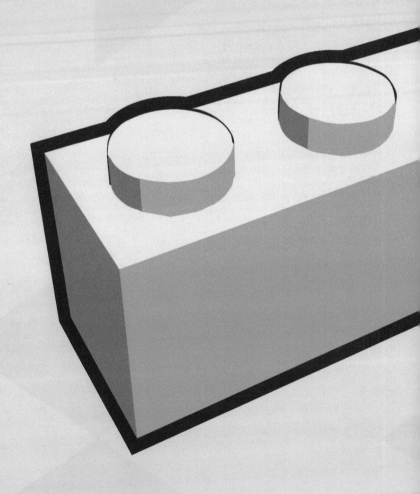

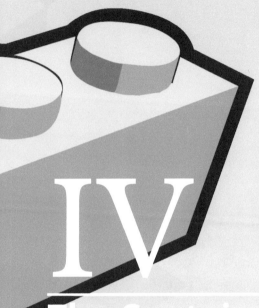

IV

The Containerization Continuum

\\. While namespaces are used to decouple applications from the operating system, the concept of namespaces itself is more broadly applicable and helps reason about application interfaces and virtualization. Particularly, namespaces are always defined with respect to the provider of resources and the interface through which the provider delivers those resources. The resources and their references used in the interface indicate the resource namespaces required to resolve potential dependencies. In case of containers, it is the kernel that provides system resources through the kernel interface. The namespaces correspond to each system resource exposed through that interface.

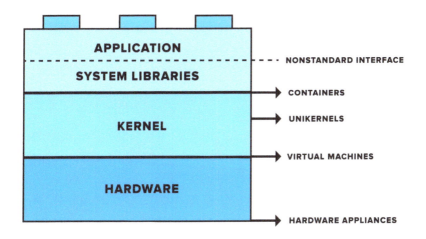

Figure 5. Boundaries at which various encapsulation approaches are implemented

The boundary around the application and the namespaces required to implement it could have been defined along other interface boundaries as well. Figure 5 shows a schematic of the typical software/hardware stack and indicates the interface layers at which virtualization can be applied. Higher level application interfaces such as the *libc* interface are not standardized as is the kernel interface, so they may be inconsistent across the various environments in which the application containers are expected to run.

Chroot, Jails and the CLONE_NEWNS Artifact

Tools such as *chroot, jails* and file system namespaces mostly encapsulate the application's file system state. They don't solve the application dependency problem because they have been created primarily as convenience file system utilities. Although these tools are useful as utilities, they don't provide a comprehensive model as required to address the application state holistically.

Early on, Linux adopted the concept of file system namespace by providing the ability to disassociate a newly created thread from the file system namespace of the parent through an extension to the thread creation system call, `clone()`. The new flag was simply called *CLONE_NEWNS* with no reference to the file system resource it disassociates because namespace at the time implicitly referred to file system namespace. The container notion was not yet introduced. Eventually, several flags were added, such as *CLONE_NEWPID*, and *CLONE_NEWNET*, each representing the respective resource. However, the original *CLONE_NEWNS* flag still remains in effect as an artifact of backward-compatibility.

Unikernels

The container boundary around an application decouples it from underlying system dependencies. However, to achieve a deeper level of isolation, some of the state within the operating system itself must be privatized for each container and included within its boundary. Unikernels do that by decomposing the operating system kernels into subsystems and directly linking relevant pieces of the kernel into the application. Application system calls then become simple calls to the operating system "functions" within their own memory address space. The state associated with these functions is private to the application and independent of other containers that include their own private state for their subsystems. The resulting isolation prevents any vulnerability in the application or linked operating system code from impacting other applications. Also, because only relevant portions of the kernel are included, the attack surface is minimized at a modest increase in application size. A major shortcoming, however, is that the approach does not work for existing applications. These applications have to be adapted to the new Unikernel model.

Virtual Machines

Virtual machines use the hardware interface to virtualize the application. In fact, they implement resource namespaces as well. These resource namespaces correspond to hardware resources such as CPUs, physical memory, and devices. Virtualizing resources at that low a level naturally encompasses all of the higher level application state. In addition to the application state, VMs also include the state of the entire operating system running underneath it. This gives virtual machines a higher degree of isolation and independence from the underlying platform. However, the additional state introduces problems such as greater startup and runtime overhead, lack of application level transparency, and higher licensing and maintenance costs. The next chapter examines virtual machines more closely.

Note that hardware appliances also provide an approach to state encapsulation. In fact, they represent the most self-contained abstractions in that they include the application as well as surrounding software and hardware, all built into a single unit.

V

Virtual Machines and Their Unwelcome Guests

"All problems in computer science can be solved by another level of indirection, except of course for the problem of too many indirections"

-- David Wheeler

Even though VMs have been used to manage traditional applications for a long time, a number of reasons make them unsuitable for the emerging class of scale-out applications where containers are
preferred.

Performance

Resources consumed by the virtualization layer can become a significant factor in the overhead equation. While resource overhead may not be a deciding factor for traditional applications, it's a different story for large distributed applications. Here the resource cost compounds quickly. The amount of host memory lost in each node of a scale-out cluster represents a huge waste of capacity. Furthermore, the high resource usage of VMs obviates dense configurations. Consequently, a physical machine is limited in the number of VMs it can run.

The high startup latency of VMs creates a major source of overhead. Unlike conventional applications that start up once and keep running, emerging environments often run short-lived tasks. The average task of a highly parallelized large job typically runs for only a short period of time, so it's unacceptable to spend an additional substantial fraction of that time bringing up the VM.

Optimization While hardware features can mitigate the overhead of CPU virtualization, overhead continues to be a problem for I/O-centric workloads. In the case of Hadoop, for example, the virtualized I/O stack consists of HDFS, guest file system, guest driver, virtual device, image format interpreter, host file system, host driver, and physical device. The aggregate overhead is significant as compared to native execution.

Interestingly, experiments measuring the performance of jobs on a distributed framework, such as Hadoop running on VMs, can be misleading. A poorly placed job on native hardware may appear to run faster when moved to virtual infrastructure. However, this seeming improvement is due to the higher overall utilization across the job rather than a speed up of individual tasks enabled by virtualization. After all, correctly tuned jobs are ultimately limited by the resources available on the underlying hardware.

Application-Hypervisor Hide and Seek

Traditionally, applications and operating systems have been built to work with each other. In a virtualized application context, the hypervisor serves a role analogous to that of the traditional operating system that manages real hardware. In doing so, it disrupts the application/OS symbiosis in that it places an opaque virtualization layer between the two. In fact, the host, guest, and hypervisor collectively perform a subset of the traditional operating system functions. Whether it's a type-A or type-B hypervisor doesn't matter. In the case of Xen, for example, the Xen kernel is the hypervisor, Dom0 is the host, and DomUs run the guests. On Linux, Linux itself is the host and Qemu/KVM is the hypervisor that in turn runs the guest kernels. Multiple layers of software performing low-level system functions can break existing application interfaces in subtle ways.

Applications running in a VM lack visibility into the topology and configuration of the underlying physical resources. What may appear to the application as a directly-attached block device may actually be a file residing on a remote NFS server.

"What may appear to the application as a directly-attached block device may actually be a file residing on a remote NFS server."

Obfuscating network and compute topologies compromises application-level resource scheduling. In the case of Hadoop, the resource manager would make suboptimal scheduling decisions based on an incorrect view of physical resources. Data and task locality may be lost, or worse yet, block replicas may end up on the same fault domain, leading to data loss.

In addition, the hypervisor lacks visibility into the application. The resulting coarse view of resources without their application-level semantic information precludes many optimizations. For example, reading a specific *config* value from a file translates into a block device read at the virtual hardware level. Without the semantic context, optimizations such as prefetching and caching would not be effective. As another example, the hypervisor reserves large portions of physical memory even when it is not used by the guest application, simply because it cannot detect unused pages within the guest.

Maintainability

Large numbers of VMs and their guest operating systems create high management burden. Promptly applying security patches to every VM across a highly dynamic infrastructure in which VMs are created and deleted on the fly can be a daunting task. VM sprawl is an additional problem. In addition to increasing the difficulty of management, the cost of guest operating system licenses can compound capex cost, especially for scale-out applications

Undue Coupling Between Application and Operating System

Virtualization is often viewed as a way to decouple applications from the underlying hardware. However, virtualization introduces new coupling between applications and their guest operating systems. Applications have to be run as VM appliances and that requires the guest operating system to be bundled into the image black box. It may be possible to migrate the entire VM, such as for hardware maintenance, but it's not possible to upgrade the operating system without disrupting the running application.

Because an application is tied to its guest operating system, the resources allocated to the application cannot be scaled on demand. Resources must first be added to the guest operating system to make them available to the application. However, guest operating systems typically require a reboot in order for additional resources such as memory or added cores to be recognized.

VMs: WRONG ABSTRACTION FOR APPLICATIONS

In the end, businesses want to run applications and not operating systems or virtual machines. It is ultimately the application that must be virtualized. Unlike containers, VMs cannot directly virtualize applications. As Figure 6 illustrates, they require a guest operating system to bridge the gap.

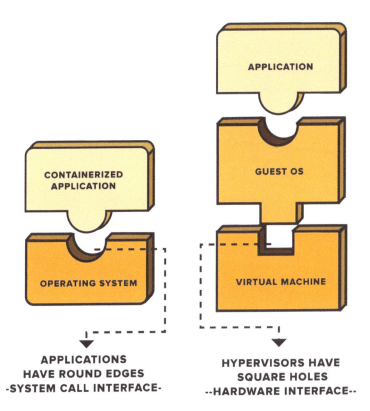

Figure 6. Virtual machines require an additional guest OS layer to virtualize the application

Over the years, industry and research communities have dedicated much collective effort in addressing the problems associated with VMs. Numerous innovations have been proposed. Some have even evolved into technologies in their own right. Unfortunately, much of this innovation does not move the state of the art forward relative to containers. Instead, it addresses the issues raised by VMs.Consequently, a large segment of the industry has been fighting the wrong battle, that is, optimizing VMs instead of applications. The problem is that optimization is limited because it's based on a fundamentally broken model. The following examples present some of the widely-adopted techniques that have been developed to circumvent the application/VM misalignment.

"A large segment of the industry has been fighting the wrong battle, that is, optimizing VMs instead of applications."

Paravirtualization

Paravirtualization is one of the most pervasive approaches developed to improve VM performance. Because the hypervisor cannot directly see or influence the guest operating system and its applications, it relies on the guest operating system to give hints or perform actions on its behalf. The interface between the guest OS and the hypervisor is called the paravirtualization API or hypercall interface. The problem is that this approach does not work with standard operating systems. It requires nontrivial changes to the kernel and the changes must be carried forward across its changing versions.

Ballooning

Operating system kernels are highly judicious with respect to committing physical memory. Through a combination of techniques (such as lazy allocation and copy-on-write), memory requests are deferred until absolutely needed. A technique called *ballooning* is used to circumvent the hypervisor's inability to access the guest operating system's internals. A ballooning driver is deployed within the guest to identify unused memory regions and convey that data back to the hypervisor. The driver squeezes out unused pages from the guest and makes them available to the host. Unfortunately, it has the side effect of periodically subjecting applications to artificial memory pressure. Although ballooning does offers somewhat of a solution, it's far less optimal than native kernel mechanisms that centrally arbitrate memory.

Deduplication

Running multiple instances of the same guest operating system and its standard services within the private memory address space of each VM causes some content to be stored across multiple memory pages. To reduce the resulting memory overhead, an online page deduplication technique called *kernel same-page merging* (KSM) has been developed. However, it imposes significant performance overhead, especially for hosts that are not memory-constrained and use non-uniform memory access (NUMA) configurations.

Undoing the Blackbox

VMs treat file system data as monolithic image blobs that are left to the guest file system to interpret. Several efforts have been expended to expose the internal structure of the opaque VM images for such operations as indexing, deduplication, and offline concurrent patching of base images, but dealing with the idiosyncrasies of image formats, their device partitions, their file systems, and their changing on-disk structures has made keeping up a nontrivial effort.

CONTAINERS: SCALED-IN VIRTUALIZATION FOR SCALE-OUT APPLICATIONS

A virtual machine provides a virtual hardware interface that can run an operating system. A container, on the other hand, provides a virtual operating system interface that can run applications. Container technology decouples the application from its environment. It creates a consistent virtual interface of the operating system by virtualizing the well-defined and semantically-rich application/OS interface as opposed to the OS/hardware interface.

As discussed earlier, a container consists of a set of namespaces. Each namespace exposes a subset of host resources to the application through their virtual names. Compute resources are virtualized by the *process* namespace. Network resources are virtualized by the *network* namespace. A virtual file system view is provided through the *mount* namespace. Since containerized processes run natively on the host under the control of the virtualization layer, the subsystems to which container virtualization is applied can be adjusted to meet the needs of the specific use case. For example, a containerized application can be confined to its private view of the file system but still be allowed to access host's network.

In contrast to virtual machines, the absence of a guest operating system layer makes containers extremely lightweight, reduces complexity, avoids duplication of functionality, and removes the overhead of intermediate layers. As a result, containers have virtually imperceptible runtime overhead and startup latency while at the same time offering orders of magnitude higher scalability and simplified management.

VI

Future of Containers: From Hype Back to Reality

II. I recently joined Raymie Stata and my former Altiscale colleagues at the Computer History Museum for a private showing of the 1960's era IBM 1401. It was an impressive experience. The different components of the imposing machine spread across the substantial demo floor. The machine chugged away for several minutes executing a simple program from a deck of punched cards. As the program completed execution, a dot-matrix printer slowly cranked out the results with the sound of a halting locomotive. Despite its size and slow speed, the 1401 looked like any modern machinery, that is until Ken Ross pried open one of the floor tiles, exposing the mess of fat interconnecting cables that ran through the subfloor interconnecting the various machine components. That's when I realized that I was observing a "compusaur".

We've come a long way since then. Through a reiterative process of encapsulating more and more complexity into well-defined modules, computers have evolved from interconnected collections of physically separate components to today's devices that model aesthetics into their design. Individual components and their interconnections are encapsulated in silicon chips. Fat cables are replaced with tiny etched lines of copper on circuit boards that model higher-level structures. The evolution continues in software. Unruly graph of system dependencies that we call applications today are not unlike complex interconnections among the components of the past computing machinery.

"Unruly graph of system dependencies that we call applications today are not unlike complex interconnections among the components of the past computing machinery."

Containers address this problem of complex interconnections through a fundamental OS abstraction designed to encapsulate software complexity into well-defined modules.

To draw another parallel, containers are to applications what file systems are to data. They define and organize applications. Data could be directly stored and retrieved to/from sectors on a storage device. However, standardization of data format in the form of file abstraction transformed information storage, retrieval and processing. File systems are so ubiquitous and intrinsic to computing substrate that they are treated as tangible entities rather than the virtualized abstractions they are. We have been writing applications as arbitrary collections of binaries, libraries and low level system interfaces with fragile interdependencies. Standardization of these software components into well-behaved modular units of logic in the form of containers will have a similar impact on applications.

MICROSERVICES: CONTAINERS ALL THE WAY DOWN

Microservices represent a further stage in the evolution of software. They enable complex application and service circuitry to be cleanly built by combining well-defined modular pieces. As illustrated in Figure 7, applications are modeled by combining containers that have well-defined external interfaces with other containers to form higher-order application services. Each container and the functionality that it encapsulates in such an ecosystem is referred to as a microservice. Combining containers of a many-tiered application service is analogous to interconnecting integrated circuit chips on a circuit board.

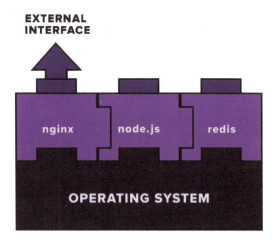

Figure 7. A typical composition of microservices that forms an application

Microservice architecture has compelling advantages. Each service can be implemented as a container independent of the rest of the application, using tools that are best suited to the task. Individual containers can be seamlessly upgraded as long as the upgraded container supports the same interface as the one it replaces. Because a microservice is a self-sufficient piece of functionality delivered as a container, a single cohesive team can assume end-to-end responsibility for its development and operation in production, leading to improved organizational effectiveness.

ROLE OF CONTAINERS IN DATA CENTER OPERATING SYSTEMS

Mapping microservices to the computing resources of a data center is an important and challenging problem. Emerging cloud-native applications built from containerized services deployed to a shared pool of cloud resources require a layer of software that offers system functions common across the applications. Systems such as Kubernetes, Mesos, YARN, and Swarm are emerging to provide that layer. Each of these systems has evolved in a unique way. Kubernetes represents Google's context of resource management at scale. YARN originated in a more data-centric batch application context. But a common thread that runs through all these systems is the container abstraction.

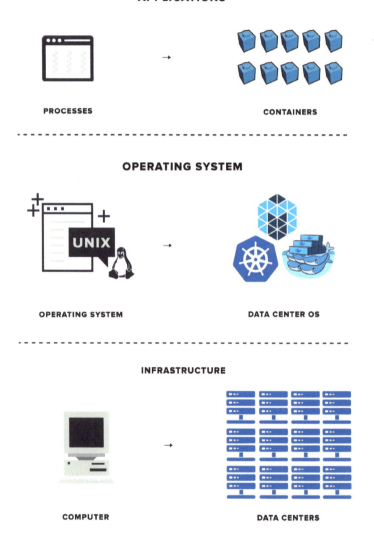

Figure 8: Containers serve as OS processes in emerging data center operating systems

Mapping microservices to the computing resources of a data center is an important and challenging problem. Emerging cloud-native applications built from containerized services deployed to a shared pool of cloud resources require a layer of software that offers system functions common across the applications. Systems such as Kubernetes, Mesos, YARN, and Swarm are emerging to provide that layer. Each of these systems has evolved in a unique way. Kubernetes represents Google's context of resource management at scale. YARN originated in a more data-centric batch application context. But a common thread that runs through all these systems is the container abstraction.

As Figure 8 illustrates, containers serve the role of processes in data center operating systems (DCOSs). Like a process in a traditional operating system that defines a task unit with a private virtualized view of basic resources, a container acts as a functional unit that encapsulates all required application state within the distributed and heterogeneous context of the data center.

To efficiently perform system level tasks in a DCOS requires equivalents of low-level OS techniques. For example, the scheduler in a traditional OS tries to maintain affinity between a process and its CPU to avoid translation lookaside buffer (TLB) flushes and cache misses. Similarly, a DCOS scheduler uses a set of locality metrics to maintain affinity between a container and the underlying node in which it runs. Due to scheduling constraints, an OS scheduler occasionally migrates a process by checkpointing its state from one CPU and restoring it to another.

For a single process, the state is small and consists mostly of the CPU register state. For efficient resource management, a DCOS must be capable of migrating a container from one node to another. For stateless containers, this migration is achieved by simply terminating the container on the source node and restarting it on the destination node. Stateful applications, however, require live migration.

Fortunately, the foundational notion of containers makes some of these primitives possible. Once the state of the application is bounded within a well-defined container abstraction, several sophisticated techniques such as checkpoint-restore, live-migration, and record/replay are possible.

CONTAINER RUNTIMES

Realizing the long-term promise of containers hinges on the standardization of the container format that represents the application and the API that exposes the core container functionality. It is the standardization of file abstraction and the filesystem API more than the richness of the filesystem feature set that has transformed the information ecosystem. Fortunately, the industry is converging on a standard. The standard is facilitating two near-term usage models.

Standardized Conduit Between Dev and Ops

Bridging the traditional gap between the development and operations teams in a typical service organization is perhaps the most rapidly growing use case. The development team produces product artifacts that the operations team is responsible for running in production. Prior to containers, the path from development to production was fraught with friction. Dev and ops environments generally tend to be quite different. The state available in the development context may be missing in production, causing the application to fail. There has been no mutually accepted medium of application delivery.

"Because containers encapsulate all required application dependencies into an immutable unit, they serve as a predictable conduit for delivering applications to the operations team."

Because containers encapsulate all required application dependencies into an immutable unit, they serve as a predictable conduit for delivering applications to the operations team. Consequently, containers, which are portable representations of applications, are emerging as the preferred medium of software distribution across organizations.

Greener VMs

Because containers project a complete virtual operating system environment, one of their natural applications is to use them as highly efficient and lightweight virtual machines. Traditional virtual machine use cases, such as server consolidation and multi-tenant cloud infrastructure, can be served far more effectively with containers. With their low runtime overhead and their fast start-up that approaches interactive timescales, containers make possible new usage models such as running short, burst tasks within isolated environments. In low-power environments such as mobile devices, low-resource footprint of containers is particularly attractive.

Isolation is a key requirement for these use cases and containers provide the required level of isolation. Containers are often used to isolate software dependencies. For example, containers allow multiple conflicting versions of the same application to be deployed on the same host. The physical resources assigned to each container can be limited to confine tenant containers to their preallocated share of underlying resources. These resource limits can be dynamically scaled up or down without bringing down the container or the application. A combination of existing mandatory access control mechanisms, recent kernel features such as private user namespaces, and potential hardware assisted container isolation mechanisms can make containers sufficiently secure.

Looking Ahead

Containers as a technology and ecosystem is in its nascent stages. There are still many capability gaps that create ample opportunity for innovation. There is room for at least several new technologies and companies to emerge in this space.

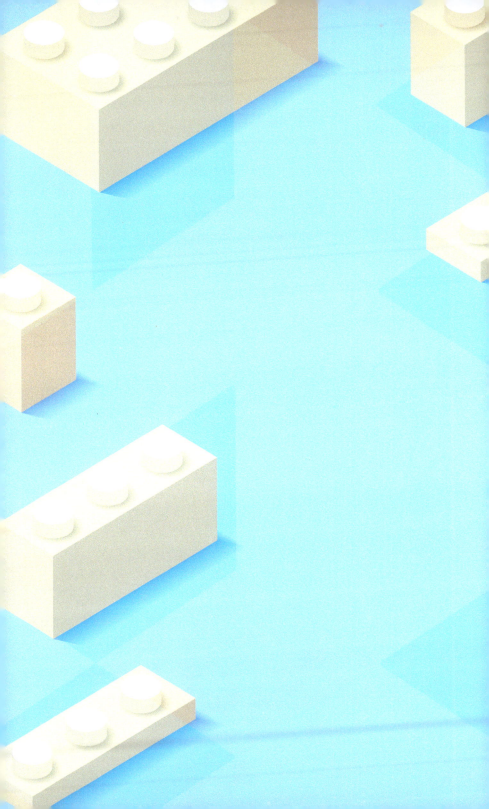

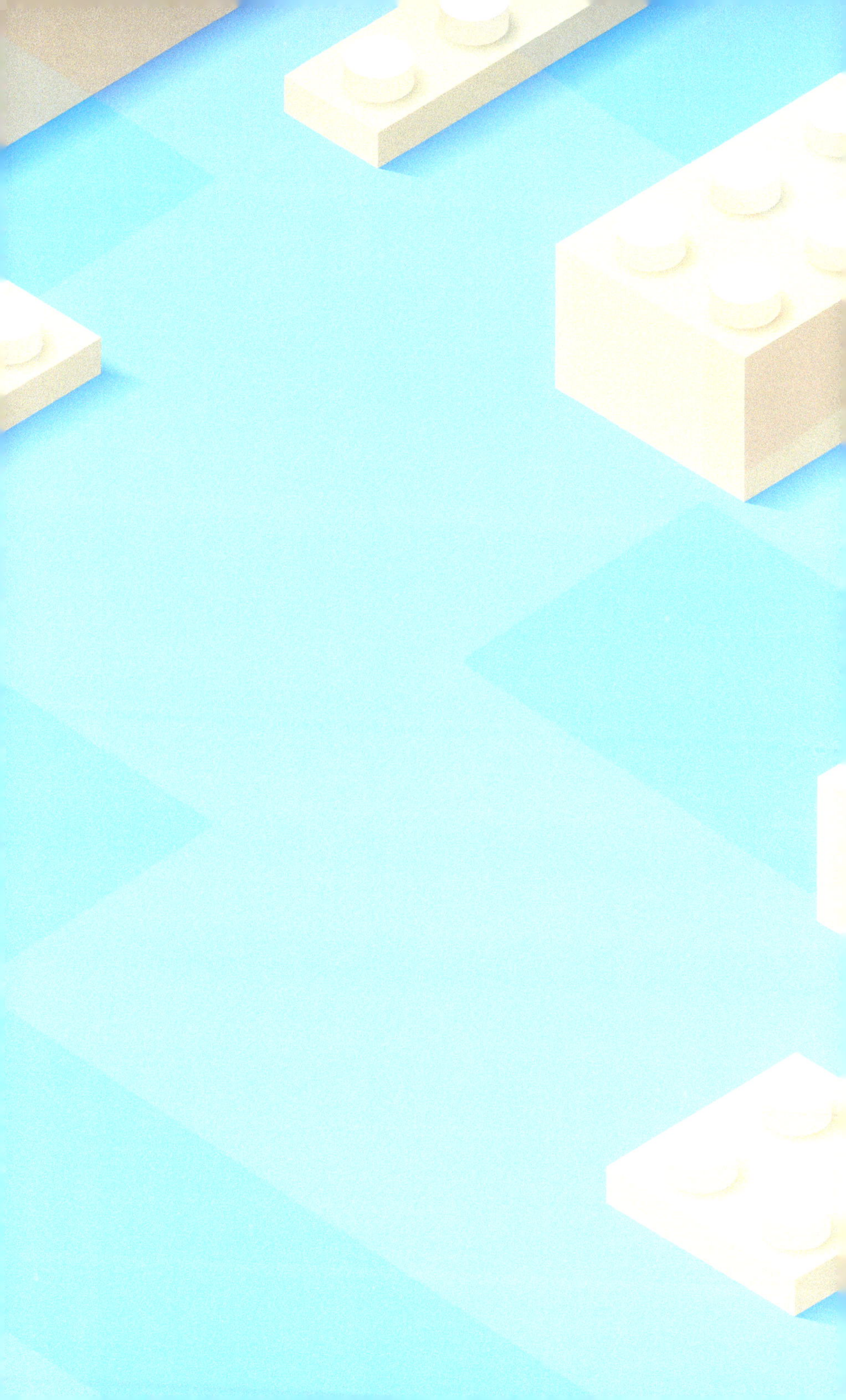